Your Amazing Itty Bitty How to Buy a Home Book

15 Steps to Achieving Home Ownership With Real Estate Education

Buying a home builds net worth, credit, tax deductions, equity, and appreciation. It can help you create stability for the long term. Buying a home gives you freedom.

The process of home buying can be daunting to those unfamiliar with it. However, don't be deterred when you find out what goes into it.

In this Itty Bitty® book, Kathryn Springsteen easily walks you through the process of home buying with steps that include:

- Financials to prepare before buying.
- How to find a good Realtor® and lender.
- Deciding where you want to buy.

If you are in the market to buy a house, now or in the future, this Amazing Itty Bitty® book is a must read.

Your Amazing Itty Bitty® How to Buy a Home Book

15 Steps to Achieving Home Ownership with Real Estate Education

Kathryn K. Springsteen, M.Ed.
Realtor®
CA DRE License 01990881

Published by Itty Bitty® Publishing
A subsidiary of S & P Productions, Inc.

Copyright © 2020 **Kathryn K. Springsteen, M.Ed.**

Printed in the United States of America

Itty Bitty Publishing
311 Main Street, Suite D
El Segundo, CA 90245
(310) 640-8885

ISBN: 978-1-950326-54-9

Dedication Page

This Itty Bitty® How to Buy a Home Book is dedicated to my broker and friend, Angelica Smith, who has been an inspiration and high achiever in her real estate field. She has taught me how to become a better than average Realtor® and helped me to achieve more than I thought I could.

Stop by our Itty Bitty® website Directory to find interesting Home Buying information from our experts.

www.IttyBittyPublishing.com

Or visit our Experts at:

www.kathrynspringsteen.com

Table of Contents

Step 1.   Buying vs. Renting
Step 2.   Financial Steps to Prepare Before
          Buying
Step 3.   How to Find a Good Lender
Step 4.   How to Find a Good Realtor®
Step 5.   Deciding Where to Buy
Step 6.   How Much House Do You Need?
Step 7.   How to Get a Pre-qualification Letter
Step 8.   What Goes into a Contract or Offer
Step 9.   Home Inspection Process
Step 10. Contingencies and Appraisals
Step 11. How to Find Hazard Insurance
Step 12. Signing Documents and Closing
Step 13. Recording and Moving In
Step 14. Investing
Step 15. Mail and Utilities

Introduction

In order to ease the stress of my clients, I decided to write this Itty Bitty® book to be a guide for what goes into buying a home.

The process can be daunting to those unfamiliar with it, and if you don't have time to learn the process or read long books you may not go through with your dream of buying your first home. You may be deterred when you find out what goes into it.

Don't lose hope. This book is designed to inform and educate the future you, a future homeowner, to prepare for the process and improve your life with home ownership.

Author's note: Several experts were interviewed for each step to ensure each topic was covered thoroughly.

Kathryn K. Springsteen, M.Ed.
Realtor®
CA DRE License 01990881

Step 1
Buying vs. Renting

Most people would like to buy rather than rent; however, in certain cases renting could fit your needs better.

1. Buying a home builds net worth, credit, tax deductions, equity, and appreciation.
2. Buying a home can help you create stability for the long term, which is great for a family or a long-term job.
3. Buying a home gives you the freedom to renovate, remodel, or update your home.
4. Renting makes it easier to move if your job requires it. Working for the military and working for the airlines are a couple of examples of jobs that require flexibility.
5. Renting is good for people who are paying off debt or building credit while saving for a down payment on their first home.
6. Renting gives you the freedom of not doing maintenance on your home other than cleaning and yard upkeep. Landlords are responsible for repairs.
7. Renting has no property taxes.

FOR RENT

Definitions for Understanding Terms in #1

These terms need to be understood when buying a house, building credit, or filing taxes.

- **Net worth** is a value of assets owned minus the debts owed. Debt-to-income ratio is a similar term used by lenders to assess value and whether a buyer can afford a loan.
- **Credit** is a score built up by using credit wisely and paying on time without having too high a debt-to-income ratio. Huge credit card debt cuts into what you will get as a mortgage.
- **Tax Deductions** and home mortgage interest are itemized, which can be deducted from your income tax return if you check with your accountant.
- **Equity** is the money you have paid on the principal (what is owed) on your home mortgage.
- **Appreciation** is what builds over time when the market increases and adds value to your home. This is the opposite of depreciation.

Step 2
Financial Steps to Prepare Before Buying

To keep your options open it is important to work on these goals to prepare for your future and to stay out of financial trouble when deciding to rent or purchase a home.

1. Pay off debts to improve debt-to-income ratio and build your credit score.
2. Build credit by using it wisely; see a credit counselor for advice.
3. Save money for a down payment on your first home; 3% to 20% of purchase price is usually needed. Be mindful that Private Mortgage Insurance (PMI) will be added if your down payment is below 20%.
4. Show income and stability when staying in a career for at least 2 years.
5. File your taxes on time, and be ready to share the tax returns with the financial lender.

How to Build Your Credit Score and Pay Down Debt.

Common ways to improve debt-to-income ratio and build credit:

- Pay off higher interest debts first.
- Make payments on time.
- Use your credit wisely or lose it.
- Not using any credit can cause poor credit scores.
- Keep balances under 30% of the total available on the credit card. Under 10% is even better.
- Having credit for a longer time can boost credit scores as well. Don't close your cards. Use them occasionally to keep them open.
- Have several accounts.
- Don't make too many hard inquiries.
- Check your credit scores once a year to maintain your scores and correct any errors by writing to the 3 credit bureaus (Transunion, Equifax, and Experian).

Step 3
How to Find a Good Lender

It is good to look for a lender who is relatively local and familiar with local laws and county taxes and requirements. Get referrals from Realtors® and friends who had their deals close quickly and smoothly. Lenders who work closely with you and your Realtor® from start to finish will help you get where you need to be to close the deal.

1. Make sure your credit is in good standing and debts are low.
2. Compare mortgage interest rates.
3. Check how much lenders charge for closing costs. Some lenders and title companies are higher than others and charge new loan fees.
4. Look at your choices between mortgage lenders, banks, private lenders, and seller-financed options.
5. You will need to provide all of your financial information to your lender and give them the required documentation for the lender to give you a pre-approval letter for your purchase offer. This is necessary as many Realtors® require a pre-approval letter before working with you.

More About Finding a Lender

The lender will need documents from you, the buyer, to submit a loan package to obtain a mortgage loan.

- Loan package submitted.
- Appraisal is ordered to establish property value.
- Underwriters review the loan.
- The Closing Disclosure (CD) and buyer's funds are sent to the escrow officer at the title company a few days before closing escrow.

Hazard and/or Fire Insurance needs to be established during escrow. In required areas, Flood Insurance will be needed as well.

- Realtors® and lenders work with buyers and insurance agents in finding what insurance is required.
- Comparing prices and coverage areas are very important.

Step 4
How to Find a Good Realtor®

A Good Realtor® is one who cares about people and wants to ensure their success in selling or buying a property. They have experience with, or they may work closely with a Broker or other Realtor® and Transaction Coordinator (TC) who can check the paperwork to see that all documents are properly signed and recorded.

1. Quantity of years in the business does not always equal Quality. One Realtor® can sell one house a year for 30 years and another can sell a house a week in 3 years. In this case, the newer Realtor® has more experience in recent years.
2. Big Franchise names do not mean they provide better service, sometimes they can be costlier, so work with a person rather than just the business.
3. Ask friends, family, or people in your local community for referrals to the best Realtors® in your area. Some Realtors® work in a small local area and some will travel farther. Most are licensed in one state, but they can refer you to agents or Realtors® in others.

Differences between Sales Agents, Realtors®, and Brokers

Brokers have an agency or firm that employs or hires independent contractors like Realtors® or real estate agents to work for the brokerage or company. The Brokers are also licensed Realtors®.

- Brokers hold more liability
- Brokers make a percentage from the sale
- Brokers pay the sales agent or Realtor®
- Brokers manage the company

A Realtor® belongs to the National Association of Realtors (N.A.R.).

A sales agent or real estate agent can only be a Realtor® if they pay the annual fees to belong to the N.A.R and they hold a state Realtors® license.

Step 5
Deciding Where to Buy

People are unique in their needs in deciding
where to buy a home. Several questions need to
be answered.

1. Have you decided what type of weather
   you prefer?
2. Do you want to be near family members?
3. Do you want to live in rural areas
   (country and farm), small town,
   suburban, or urban (city) areas?
4. What type of career do you have, and
   where do you need to live to be
   successful?
5. Are you looking for a primary home or
   investment home?
6. Do you have pets or children or other
   relatives living with you to consider?
7. Do you need to be near schools, work,
   churches, parks, community centers?
8. Do you require public transportation?

Places to Look for Houses to Buy or Rent

Here are places to start looking for a place once you have decided to purchase or rent a home.

- Ask your local Realtor® to add you to the local MLS, Multiple Listing Service, for email updates.
- Internet Search
- Realtor.com
- Your Local Newspaper
- Drive around and look at the area.
- Find "For Sale" signs.

Step 6
How Much House Do You Need?

Many times, people buy more house than they need or can afford to maintain. First time home buyers may be better off with a smaller, starter home. The buyers may live there for a couple of years for tax benefits and then sell in a high market if they need more space or want to upgrade. Things to consider:

1. Affordability
2. Square footage
3. Bedrooms
4. Bathrooms
5. Yard or acreage
6. Fencing
7. Shop, shed, garage, or barn
8. Yearly tax assessments
9. School district if children are involved

Reasons to Upsize or Downsize

These are common reasons to upsize or move to a larger home.

- Growing family
- Pet space
- Feeling cramped
- Need office space for home business
- Need a hobby or exercise room
- Need guest rooms
- Entertaining large groups

These are common reasons to downsize or move to a smaller home.

- Children have grown up and moved out
- Fewer needs
- Feels more cozy
- Lower payments (mortgage, utilities, taxes, etc.)
- Less house to clean and upkeep

Step 7
How to Get a Pre-qualification Letter

General items are needed for a lender to provide a
pre-qualification letter. These items may vary
according to the lender.

1. Driver's License or Photo ID
2. Social Security Card
3. Paystubs for last thirty to sixty days.
4. Federal tax returns for the last two years
   including any 1099 or W-2's or Schedule
   C forms for the self-employed.
5. Bank statements for last two months.
6. Residential addresses over last two years.
7. Landlord's contact information for last
   two years.
8. List of all financial accounts including
   retirement or stocks.
9. List of all income.
10. List of all revolving debts and credit
    accounts.
11. List of liens or collections against you.
12. Down payment information and source of
    income.
13. Employment and Employer information.
14. Income history.

IMPORTANT Tips to Remember to Qualify for a Mortgage - Pitfalls to Avoid

During the process of buying a home or during the escrow period, DO NOT DO ANY OF THESE THINGS, OR YOU CAN JEOPARDIZE YOUR LOAN APPROVAL!

- Do not open OR close any credit card accounts.
- Do not move large amounts of money from one account to another.
- Do not make any large purchases.
- Do not change jobs.
- Do not move your mailing address if possible. You may miss something important.
- Don't buy furniture yet. Wait until after escrow is closed and it records.

Step 8
What Goes into a Contract or Offer

Several things go into a contract, offer, or purchase agreement. Realtors® use their state association of Realtors® documents or forms, and they explain the process.

1. Name of Seller or Sellers on Title
2. Name of Buyer or Buyers
3. Address of Property
4. Assessor's Parcel Number (APN#)
5. Date of Offer and Close of Escrow
6. Agency Disclosure - Agency Representation.
7. Amount of Earnest Money Deposited
8. Amount of Down Payment
9. Purchase Price
10. Type of Financing or Cash
11. Contingencies, Verification, and Loan Terms
12. Items included and excluded in or on property. Items attached permanently to the walls, like drapes, normally stay.
13. Allocation of Costs and Inspections
14. Disclosures, Time Periods, Dispute Resolution
15. Acceptance or Counter or Rejection
16. Initials on each page with Signatures and Dates.

FOR
SALE

When in Contract…

Once the offer is accepted the property goes into contract or is pending escrow. The escrow officer at a title company, or a real estate attorney in some states, handles the transfer of title.

- Preliminary report and inspections are ordered by the escrow officer or attorney and Realtor®.
- Realtors® have buyers, and sellers sign disclosures.
- Lenders begin to submit the documents collected from the buyers.

Every state and agency have a similar, but sometimes different process.

- Check with your Realtor®, Lender, Escrow Officer, Attorney, Accountant, and Insurance Agent for what is needed during the property purchasing process in your state.

Step 9
Home Inspection Process

Buyers decide with their Realtors® or Brokers which inspections they need. Lenders also will tell them which inspections are required for the type of loan they are getting. These are common inspections done during the escrow period.

1. Whole House Inspection.
2. Pest Inspection.
3. Well Inspection
4. Septic Pumping and Inspection
5. Roof Inspection

Sometimes buyers have a valid reason to select more inspections and surveys. Each inspection can add to the buyer's cost, so only those really needed are usually done.

Home warranties are also recommended by the real estate broker. The warranty company can cover repairs to some items like appliances, plumbing, electrical, roofing, air conditioner, furnace, septic, etc. Check what you would like covered by the warranty or sign a waiver if you choose not to get a warranty.

Repairs may be needed.

The inspections may show items that require repairs for a loan approval. This can be stressful for everyone involved. The buyer's Realtor® will submit a request for repairs and negotiate with the listing agent and sellers. Sellers may, or may not, decide to pay for repairs. You would benefit by checking if there are any warranties that will cover repairs as well, such as a home warranty.

If the items affect structure and safety, they will need repairs. Paint and type of floor coverings are not generally considered a repair, even though these items may need to be repaired.

- Dry rot
- Pest removal
- Well or Septic repairs
- Roof repairs or certification
- Appliance repairs
- Plumbing repairs
- Electrical repairs
- Smoke detector/carbon monoxide detector installation
- Heater installation
- Other repairs

Step 10
Contingencies

Contingencies are safety checks for the buyer to be able to opt out of the contract to purchase a property. These contingencies are common, but more can be put into an initial offer if needed.

1. Inspection period
2. Appraisal
3. Loan approval

The inspection period varies by state, and it can be changed on the offer or on an addendum if you're waiting for inspector appointments or repairs to be completed.

The appraisal is ordered by an independent company through the lender. They make an appointment to inspect the house and determine if it is worth the selling price. They may use three types of appraisal methods.

1. Sales comparison approach
2. Cost approach
3. Income capitalization approach.

Once the appraisal is completed the loan proceeds to the lenders who underwrite the loan. The loan usually gets approved at this juncture.

Sellers also can have Contingencies.

Sometimes the seller also has a contingency.

- Sellers may need to find a home to move to prior to closing escrow.
- Sellers may need more time to have repairs done.
- Sellers may need more time to remove cumbersome unattached property.

An extension can be filed in these cases if amicable to both sellers and buyers; however, escrow may be delayed.

Step 11
How to Find Hazard Insurance

Some areas are prone to floods, fires, hurricanes, tornadoes, and other disasters. Thus, it is important to have your home and contents covered by insurance to rebuild or buy another home if disaster strikes.

1. Check with your insurance broker.
2. Check with your local Realtor® for common companies that provide insurance.
3. You may need to settle for a state plan if the property is located in a difficult area to get insurance coverage.
4. Ask the neighbors which company they use.
5. Clear brush around the property after closing, if needed.

More About Insurance

Due to the potential of natural disasters, many insurance companies are charging more or not insuring homes in rural areas without fire clearance. Check with your insurance broker.

1. You may need to pay one year upfront.
2. Your mortgage company may have an escrow or impound account to hold your monthly insurance payments as well as your property tax payments. They will pay both payments when due.
3. Property tax, insurance, and the interest on your loan will likely be added to your monthly principal mortgage payment.

Step 12

Signing Documents and Closing

Your local title company or attorney, depending on what state you are in, will set up a closing appointment for you to sign the closing documents.

1. There are options available when you are unable to attend your closing in person. You may request a mobile notary, go to another office to sign the documents, or have the documents sent to you so that you may sign them and send them back via overnight mail to the title company.
2. Ask your Lender and Realtor® to check the estimated closing statement for any errors, additions, or omissions.
3. If your Realtor® can attend, ask them to meet you there. Some people feel more comfortable when their Realtor® is present.
4. Smile, you are almost done with the process!

SOLD

More about the Closing

The signing package from the title company will be sent to your real estate broker. The real estate agent or Realtor® will be paid a commission out of the proceeds from the broker. The real estate agent has fees, insurance, and taxes to pay out of said commission. The commission for real estate agents is generally paid for out of the seller's escrow.

The broker will keep copies of your documents for you for up to five years should you require additional copies.

Step 13
Recording and Moving In

The day you sign the closing documents is not the end of the process. The title company or real estate attorney will send the documents to your local county for recording. Sometimes the paperwork is recorded the same day, and other times it may take a few days.

1. Documents are sent to record at your county recorder's office.
2. Confirmation of recording is sent back to the title company or real estate attorney.
3. The title company or real estate attorney notifies your Realtor® who notifies you.
4. Your Realtor® gives you the keys and congratulates you.
5. Your Realtor® may give you tips on the local community and utility companies.
6. You coordinate moving in with your movers.

Moving In

There are several ways to move your personal property into the new home you just bought.

- Hire movers to pack you and deliver your belongings to your new home.
- Box everything yourself and hire movers to transport your goods.
- Rent a truck and do it yourself.
- Move your belongings in your own vehicle.
- Get friends and family to help.

Moving can be very exhausting. Drink lots of water and get plenty of rest during your move. Once the move is completed you might wish to celebrate with a massage.

Step 14
Investing

Investing in properties is how the rich get richer if done right. It also can create a huge loss if the market crashes. Here are some steps to look at if buying an investment property.

1. Choose less expensive houses through short sales, pre-foreclosures, foreclosures, probate, divorces, abandoned houses, auctions, and tax liens.
2. Buy when the market is low.
3. Sell when the market is high.
4. If selling investment property, save taxes by using a 1031 exchange. Ask your accountant for details.
5. Use the rule of 72 to determine when an investment will profit.

The **Rule of 72** is a simple way to determine how long an investment will take to double given a fixed annual rate of interest. By dividing **72** by the annual rate of return, investors obtain a rough estimate of how many years it will take for the initial investment to duplicate itself.

https://www.investopedia.com/ask/answers/what-is-the-rule-72/

More Investing Knowledge

Here are some ways to invest if you are interested in investing in real estate.

- Fix and Flip (Renovate: Buy low, fix, sell high.)
- Rentals (Use a property manager for background checks, repairs, and evictions.)
- Self-directed IRA (Invest your retirement into a self-directed IRA based on real estate.)
- Wholesale (Make money on the sale by getting into a contract and reselling to a buyer. Check the laws in your state.)
- Buy and Sell using Seller-financed notes. (Become the bank.)

Here are some ideas shared by a real estate investment group.

- Network with investors, as well as private or hard money lenders.
- Use other people's money or lenders to invest and free your cash flow.
- Use a line of credit or a self-directed IRA to purchase and fix up properties.

Step 15
Mail and Utilities

It is important to contact your prior post office requesting to have mail forwarded to your new address. This can be done in person or online at usps.com. The post office will forward your mail for up to 6 months, so you have time to update your contact information with all the companies you do business with as soon as you move into your new home.

1. Forward your mail at your post office to your new address or P.O. Box.
2. Contact new utility companies, electric, gas, water, garbage to put into your name and close your old accounts.
3. Contact phone company, both mobile and/or landlines, with your new address.
4. Contact TV, cable, satellite or Internet companies and change your services.
5. Update all banks with new address and contact information.
6. Update all creditors and debtors with new address and contact information.
7. Update any newspaper or magazine services with new address.
8. Update airline, hotel, and other travel memberships with new address.

Mail and Utilities

Another nice thing to do is to contact your family and friends with your new physical and mailing address, unless you don't want to be contacted by some of them.

- Parents
- Siblings
- Children
- Other Relatives
- Friends
- Clubs
- Churches
- Schools
- Jobs

Never be afraid to ask your professional advisors (your Realtor®, your accountant, your attorney, your insurance broker, your escrow officer, your utility companies, your mailperson, or neighbors) if you have any questions or needs.

I appreciate you taking the time to read this Itty Bitty® Book. I hope you learned something along the way. Enjoy your new home or investment property!

You've finished. Before you go...

Tweet/share that you finished this book.

Please star rate this book.

Reviews are solid gold to writers. Please take a few minutes to give us some itty-bitty feedback.

ABOUT THE AUTHOR

Kathryn Springsteen is a Realtor® for Amplify Real Estate & Properties with offices in Brownsville, Yuba City, and Rocklin, California. She works in Yuba and Sutter counties primarily. She also works in surrounding counties from Sacramento to Chico and to Grass Valley.

Springsteen has experience in buying and selling properties, in property management, and in starting and managing small businesses. She also is a Real Estate investor and educator.

Springsteen has an Interior Design Certificate, Real Estate Agent License, a Master's Degree in Education with a major in Curriculum & Instruction with a Reading Specialization, and a Multiple-Subject Teaching Credential. She also has worked with small business development and worked in a construction office.

Springsteen decided to focus on teaching during the years her four children were young. Now she is working on her other passion-helping people to find the right home for them, and assisting people to better their financial net worth through investing in real estate!

If you enjoyed this book you might also like…

- **Your Amazing Itty Bitty® Sell Your Home Book** – Eduardo Mendoza

- **Your Amazing Itty Bitty® Blissful Real Estate Investing Book** – Moneeka Sawyer

- **Your Amazing Itty Bitty® Real Estate Exam Book** – Stephanie Stern

Or any of the many other Itty Bitty® books available online at www.ittybittypublishing.com